UDDER UPROAR

UDDER UPROAR

by
Catherine Perkins

Accents Publishing • Lexington, Kentucky • 2024

Printed in the United States of America

Accents Publishing
Editor: Katerina Stoykova
Cover Design: Simeon Kondev
Cover Image: *Beef à la Mode* by Thomas Rowlandson, 1800

ISBN: 978-1-961127-05-0
First Edition

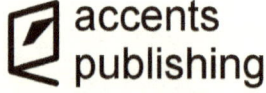

Accents Publishing is an independent press for brilliant voices. For a catalog of current and upcoming titles, please visit us on the Web at

www.accents-publishing.com

CONTENTS

To Antoinette Graven Perkins,
aka Mother,
you always wanted to write your memoirs,
but never did.
I always wanted to laugh
and do.

Life is tragedy for those who feel and comedy for those who think.

—Molière, aka Jean-Baptiste Poquelin

ODE TO MY OBESITY

O, luscious curves, you've gotten out of control,
fat from head to toe, every inch has a roll.

Bulbous belly outspreads the yawn of ample hips.
I gasp for gulps of air with open pink lips.
Snorts and grunts escape from this fat-backed human.
Fifty pounds of excess weight: blubber shakes,
quakes, makes my feet ache, fails to dissipate
no matter how hard I try to shed the freight.

Chronic hunger compels me to the cupboard.
A gluttonous gourmand, food cannot be ignored.

My hefty rump, so rotund I tilt askew,
boobs flap, labia thwap, butt cheeks flutter farts,
no body part evades chafes, even thighs abrade.
O, sweet potbelly, I know you mean well,
but hell, crumbs on the floor or breasts that sag
is a price I'd pay for less portly swag.

O, buttery obesity, set this plump frame free,
restore the good ole days of foxy, fit and firm.

I grab the bag of chocolate-covered crickets,
low-calorie and healthy if I eat a snippet,
but I consume until the bag is empty.
Dizzy, I embrace my hugeness instead,
grab a cookie, head to bed, and thank my fat
I fit through doors and am not dead.

MAMMARIES HAVE SOMETHING TO SAY

You keep us upright,
bind us up tight.

Like an underfed boa constricts
our movements you restrict.

You slow the flow of blood
to our voluptuous buds,

push up and cup for unnatural
cleavage between the pups.

The broken flesh rubs
from wires jutting into the jugs

and the bruises you infuse make us blue.
Amazing not one of us has ever sued.

Bra makers get a grip,
invent virtual lift!

*

A plucky old gal had boobs that drooped
causing her to walk bent over and stooped.
They hung to her knees,
bounced when she sneezed.
She used them to sweep poop in the coop.

THE MOST UNDER-APPRECIATED SUPERMOON
IN THE HISTORY OF SUPERMOONS

No poems or tributes ever written
about or to the huge rear on my posterior.

No photo shoots of her shooting
have been recorded for infamy.

Truth is, there's been a diverse plethora
of shapes and facades on this full-figured bottom.

Once or twice, even after this bulbous orb became
a mother's behind a headline could have read:

Supermom's Supermoon Has a Face on Her Surface.
Yet in spite of this lack of assign she continues to shine.

She's bucked, been plucked and harvested.
Wolves used to howl at her lusciousness.

She's been cold as ice on icy nights and still,
no one writes about when she smells nice.

This old butt used to hunt for lovers and good times,
now it's hard chairs and high toilets.

Like a sturgeon in August, this plump rump is an easy catch.
When young she loved to ride and run. Now older, she's much slower.

In spite of her desire to be recognized, her glory
remains unseen unless her owner's high on something.

THE COLOR OF GUILT

Injured and unable to drive
much less get outside
I force myself to try
to do things.

Wheelchair to chair,
I watch videos on how to maneuver stairs.
I one-crutch down into the basement
in search of pencils, markers, gel pens

and coloring books from my child's childhood.
Using belts around my waist
and tied to the handle of a small suitcase
I drag and pull it up steep steps.

I sit at the dining room table
and begin to color. I feel
embarrassed and disgraced
by my brokenness.

For hours I swim in indolence.
I can't stay in between the lines,
but I don't stop after the first day.
I enter a picture in a coloring contest.

I win a coloring book.
Now I'm hooked
until it's time
to learn how to walk again.

LAP DANCE

My
belly
fat
jiggles
and wiggles,
quivers
and shakes,
rolls
and rocks,
heaves
and ho-ho-ho's
when
I laugh
long
and hard,
uproarious.

HOW TO FIX A LEAK

There's a leak between my thighs.
A nemesis that keeps me inside.
    drip
    drip
    drip
They don't make gaskets to fix it.
Plugs and balls meant to tighten walls
or paddles to straddle, about all.
I search the World Wide Web
for ways to tighten up the tired old gal.
I find porn. I type in: *how to control the flow.*
I get a plethora of exercises I already know.
I don't like surprises when I cough or sneeze
and sure as hell don't want to sit
on the toilet until it quits   the
    drip
    drip
    drip
Could the reason be lack of action?
The solution more self-satisfaction.
At my age how can I rely on a helping hand
to dam the damned? The push-push
sounds like a chore, a surefire path to a sore
or torn paper-thin-wilted-skin-flower-with-no-power.
Some say there are surgical procedures:
meshes, tucks or balloons,
that might ease her seizures.
    drip
    drip-drip
    drip-drip-drip
    drip
The specialist's advice: *Use it or lose it.*
Quit thinking how, but what's next.

Your lily needs to act silly.
The pubococcygeus muscle needs exercise.
If you lack time or desire, I'll write a script
for a drug guaranteed to revive her Venus,
even make you want a penis.
The stop-leak-tweak is just one pill a day
if you decide to fix her   the easy way.

SPEED READING

Genital Yoga is what I read
as I sped along Highway 65.
I replied to my eyes
What the hell is that?
Then I began to imagine:

Yoga teacher:
Okay class, sit on the ball,
open your hips, stretch the lips,
lay on your backs, spread and relax,
tighten, release, spread, relax, tighten,
release. Repeat ten times.
Roll over.
Raise and lower your buttocks,
feet and hands on the floor,
raise, lower, raise, lower, repeat.
Don't forget to breathe.

Another billboard appeared
for the same yoga class.
Now I wasn't driving as fast.
Gentle Yoga, it said,
and I replied to my eyes
I like my yoga better.

THE JOINT IS JUMPIN'*

You belly up to the record player,
pull from the stack of LPs Billie, Benny,

Erroll, Fats and Dave. You place them on the center pin
with care. The first one drops to the turntable.

The stylus lifts from the rest and settles on the black disc.
Music seeps through the pores of the house.

This joint is jumpin' the piano's thumpin'
You shed your clothes, except brassiere and panties,

un-closet the vacuum, check its bag and start to clean.
Your feet keep beat as you swing hose and arms.

Check your weapons at the door.... Your breasts
bobble, bottom bounces, legs jitterbug, your partner

sucks dirt as you raise the volume and dust.
Dog, cat and kids hide outside for fear

of being in the way, or worse, put to work.
Sweat wets your shapely silhouette.

The tempo slows. You slide a rag to Billie's blues.
I don't know if it's tears or perspiration on your cheeks.

I watch you whirl-twirl, push-pull, huff-puff, dance and cuss
in Dutch and French. *Merde! Zut alors! Quel cochon!*

Oh, dear wild Mama on the other side of live,
I often dream a dream of you cleaning.

I hope one day to be like you, dress in lingerie or go nude,
grab Billie, Benny, Frank and Fats from the internet,

swear and sweep my home at least once a week,
sweat and tears running down my cheeks   as I remember   you.

* *The Joint is Jumpin'*, 1937. Music written by Fats Waller, lyrics by Andy Razaf, J.C. Johnson.

WHISKERS

She rubbed and rubbed and rubbed her chin
like a philosopher pondering where to begin.
She rubbed while she was awake,
six hours a day until her fingers ached.

The worry and fret massage of whiskers
started when her eyes began to see in flickers.
She couldn't see to tweeze, so she begged us (her children), *Please
shave, pull, make them leave, perhaps a chemical freeze.*

I, the "good" daughter, researched removal procedures,
all came at a cost that gave me seizures.
What I discovered, another scam uncovered,
expensive, not permanent and only works on hairs colored.

Five hundred bucks for five laser burns or deep root plucks
on a fixed income is just too much. Robbing the elderly really sucks.
Those of us sprouting beards and mustaches know,
some hairs are black, others gray bristles that barely show.

But those muthas grow like weeds overnight,
rigid slivers of steel that make a woman uptight.
Mama, I said, *rub those nubs just don't rub off your skin
because that could spell disaster for you and your kin.*

Now my whiskers daily sprout
and unless I pluck those bastards out
I rub my chin and think of Mama's face the day she died,
full of whiskers on both sides.

AGING IS NOT FOR THE MEEK

Aging is not for the meek.
The body begins falling apart.
Strange sounds escape from cheeks.

People stare like I'm a freak
as I walk past popping farts.
Aging is not for the meek.

My hair turns gray in streaks,
there's the gradual loss of smarts,
strange noises escape from my cheeks.

It takes longer and longer to peak.
Even my vibrator has a bad heart.
Aging definitely is not for the weak.

The bladder is prone to leaks.
Timing when to pee is an art.
Still they come, strange sounds from the cheeks.

If only I could hire a geek
to upgrade the motherboard's parts.
Aging is not for the meek.
Strange sounds escape from the cheeks.

ON HAVING

I have a house.
I have heat in the house.
I have air conditioning in the house.
I have running water in the climate-controlled house.
I have knick-knacks everywhere in the comfortable house
      with hot and cold running water.
I have pictures on the walls and food in the refrigerator in the cozy
      two-bathroom house filled with knick-knacks and inherited kitsch.
I have computers, TVs, radios, clocks and phones in the red brick,
      electrified, windowed, trinket-full, gray shingled-roof house.
I have a few hundred dollars in jars in the well-lit, indoor-plumbed,
      eclectically furnished house I share with my husband,
      daughter, dogs, cat and friend, who lives in the basement.
I have a car, a truck, a horse trailer, and a business
      with cards to prove it.
I have an outbuilding. I have a garage. I have a yard.
I have a garden in the yard. I have art in the garden.
I have tools that I don't know how to use.
I have toys I don't play with and books I will never read.
I have health insurance, car insurance, homeowner's insurance,
      workman's comp and liability.
I have credit cards. I have debt. I even have my own bedroom.
I have self-pity, low self-esteem, bad teeth, poor vision
      and an atrophied vagina. I have the blues.
I have pride. I have humility. I have laughter, soft bones
      and a concussed, confused brain.
I have some kindness, a touch of empathy, a little love
      and a whole lot of distrust.
I have pain. I have fear. I have honesty and I have tactlessness.
I have demons, apathy, ignorance and greed living inside of me.
I have what money can and cannot buy.
I am overstuffed and satisfied.

THE ELEPHANT CHASE

I bellowed with all my might as I ran in fright
from the angry giant trumpeting in my ears
closing in on my rear.

You see, no, I know you don't see
what happened to me so, here's the story
of how I almost died in the Serengeti.

I was walking in haste with my attention on the face
of my phone when I accidentally bumped into an elephant's
butt smacking my head onto his nuts.

The elephant, young and in musk,
to run me down, he decided, was a must.
Lucky for me my phone had Global Positioning.

It directed me to a hiding place
where I could wait while the livid bull stomped
and paced as he contemplated my fate.

What I learned that day: Mute notifications and texts
from friends, shield my eyes from GIFs and memes,
be polite and pay attention even when it's hard to resist temptation.

I was saved that summer's day by the very device
that almost caused me to lose my life.

THE CLOUDS ARE FULL

I don't understand technology these days.
I don't know how to uninstall billowy cumuli in a virtual sky,
but putting them in the trash sounds immoral and brash.

Worse yet, digital engineering
Mother Nature's state of being seems to me
downright unsustainable and misleading.

Amazon took my cirrostrati away.
They didn't tell me to where, but I care
because I don't remember what was up there.

Pop-up windows say my operating system is passé.
Apple claims my computer's too old for upgrading.
I can't locate stratiform veil passwords.

iCloud wants money for more mesosphere.
Google says there's no room in the stratosphere,
and when I try to delete what's in the atmosphere

messages appear saying my saved knowledge
will disappear. My sense of humor abates
as I watch clouds I cannot see   dissipate.

BALDERDASH

Multi-colored balloons dance like ballerinas
in the bright blue sky. Set free to fly by a balmacaan-
clad man who smells of balsam and ripe bananas.

He juggles bamboo sticks, has in tow a bandicoot,
by his side a sheathed bandoneon and a banjo
drapes shoulder to waist like a banner.

From second story windows banshees
yell at the little parade. Bantams
peck at his bare feet. Buck naked barflies

circle the barmy baron,
bathe him in bath water from the bayou
and send him off to the bazaar.

THE COCKS CRY

I rush towards the pleas for *help-help-help*.
I almost get hit by a speeding car careening
down my narrow street. I hear *help-help-help*
over there and over there and behind my back
and from the roof of a barn and from a limb of a tree. Which tree?
I can't see where all the help-hollering hes are hiding.

Two cocks indulge in simultaneous screams: *threlp-threlp*
thrrelp-thrrelp Screeches ricochet. I don't know who to seduce,
but seduce I must as I am in lust. Three seconds of silence
then a sudden burst of deep-throat rolling *rrr rrr* captures
my ears to turn my eyes to the glistening, shimmering fool
staring at his reflection in the attic window on the gray-shingled roof.

Another round of cock-caws come from a six-foot-tailed fowl
perched on a bur oak limb. He looks strong. I am as drawn
to him as he is to himself. I let him know I am near, down here
in the yard staring up at him, but he doesn't hear. To hell
with that narcissist. I switch my fascinations to the twerking
eye-filled fanny that magically appears a few feet from my face.

Thick stick-legs scratch and tap. A long arched blue neck blinds.
His flutter of feathers vibrates my cloaca. So, I stand in wait
and I wait and I wait and I wait and I whisper, *Hey, cock-on-the-block,*
I'm no ordinary peahen. I am the sole hidey-hen-hole in this hood.
Let's kiss, I hiss, but the long-tailed beauty is too busy
with his *help-help*s and dance to notice I am entranced.

Fed up with these self-absorbed cocks' antics, I chortle, *No way*
and scamper off to the other side the big white shed where a lek
of blue-necks rest. These young males have shorter tails, tinier spurs
and leaner limbs, but I am the center of four cocks' attentions.
I kiss the entire lot, yet regret the first two handsome Indian Cocks
were so in love with themselves because I could have had a perfect score.

THE LITTLE BLUE PILL

> One pill makes you larger ...
> —*White Rabbit* by Grace Slick

You know the pill,
the one that will
make the penis fill,
increase blood flow,
make heads glow, harden trees
to withstand the strongest breeze,
and enable men to copulate on any date,
no matter their mental state,
so they may spread the seed,
and yes, improve the breed.

Until

the day,
you know the day when
blindness comes (in one eye),
deafness comes (in one ear, men don't hear anyway),
depression comes (seems like coming is the theme!)
from the little blue pill
that makes the penis erect,
but doesn't make men intelligent.

But

imagine if you can
another day, a day when
one is primed to get laid.
The wood is ready.
The wood stands tall.
No amount of jerk, beat,
stroke the dog, pound the meat,
push-push in the bush, or no-bush,
will make the phallic pole fall!

Then

you have a sore and pissed-off mate,
an emergency room wait
or worse, a dick that won't deflate—
oh, the little blue pill taker's fate.
Some things are so damn funny.

ODE TO GONADS

O, tender testes I love how you hang at forks of torsos,
visible or hidden, under bellies or between flanks,

many of you so small you might not be seen at all.
Goolies that droop long, low and loose, like those on a moose,

bull, ram, possibly a man, I'll be damned
those banger balls must be blessed lest

they be beaten blue and bruised. Gonads that thwap
side to side make some critters walk kind of wide.

The cobblers of a man might fit in one hand,
two pug-sized pebbles in a palm and how's about

rocks that need cups to hold 'em up, and cryptorchids—
creatures with just one sugar plum descended

or no stone out and about? Guess what?
They can still pop a nut, knock-up.

Some drool when sampling Rocky Mountain oysters.
A student of fine dining savors succulent lamb fries.

O, sweet-soft-salty-surround-skin-of-the-scrotum,
silken-feel-to-fingers, no nut I've touched has been rough.

Huevos-melt-in-mouth-knacker-snacks make lips smack.
Colossal cojones take one's breath away. Oh, gasp.

And nards with a nipple or teat, a visual treat.
A dog's bollocks too cute trotting down the street.

O, sacs of spermatozoa, creators of characters,
tenders of temperaments, attitude adapters,

jewels, junk, easy bruisers, brawn builders,
shiny-vein-lined-downy-dusted brains, takers

of common sense, makers of nonsense, progenitors
of populations, fascinators of fascinations, thank you

for helping the world go round. Without y'all,
I wonder would the wheel have been found?

RECIPE FOR TOE FLAMBÉ

Ingredients:

1 red convertible with fancy web-spoked rims
2 freshly picked humans (one slightly older, but both of legal age)
1 tablespoon of beauty
3 cups of hair, any color, any length
3 3oz. bags of dark chocolate French kisses
1 cup equal parts of lipstick, musk, perfume, deodorant
3 pounds of salted butter—the more butter the better
1 pint whiskey

Directions:

1. Put 1 body in driver's seat of the red convertible
2. Add body 2, fully dressed, to passenger seat of said red car.
3. Drive red car to an alley. Park between two garages.
4. Rip open 1 bag of French kisses, begin to consume eagerly.
5. Unscrew top of whiskey, take small sips, gulping might make you sick. Pass bottle back and forth.
6. Set butter aside to soften.
7. Place all ingredients together, except 2 bags of French Kisses, 1 pound of soft butter and ½ pint of whiskey.
8. Stir or whisk* vigorously, making sure to blend well.** Fold in 1 bag of kisses.

* If you whisk too hard curdling will be an issue.
** Occasionally, a body will try to separate and float to the top, if this occurs, add a few shots of whiskey and stir more.

Once ingredients bind, move batter to back seat, remove shoes, smear mixture on toes using fingers, lick fingers before touching anything. Proceed to suction-clean each other's piggies adding kisses to the tips. Massage leftover softened butter onto exposed skin. Pour ample swigs of whiskey down throats, making sure to spill droplets into belly buttons, for lapping purposes.

Ignite with lust and eat until all are consumed.

FRISSON

Coitus, couple, copulate,
congress, screw, fornicate—
a few ways to say coition,
sex for fun or procreation.

Used to be the spread of thighs
brought mates ejaculations and satisfied sighs.
Love, a horny man's promise I could not resist,
yet loneliness the outcome, not bliss.

One day a friend told me the power
of bathtub spigots and shejaculating showers.
Who knew tingles, chills and thrills could come
from the nether regions of a woman?

Once complete with this carnal knowledge
they did not teach in sex-ed or college,
I began to squirt and gush,
orgasms became a selfish rush.

No friction of bodies should be complete
until all toes curl on a woman's feet,
until little buttons throb and are ticklish,
until all attendees talk to Jesus in gibberish.

MARRIAGE JOKE

my husband and I are a perfect match
neither of us has ever remembered our wedding anniversary
we hate doing paperwork
and we dislike talking

to each other

no wonder
we are still married

SUBMIT

> Now as the church submits to Christ, so also wives should submit in everything to their husbands.
>
> —Ephesians 5:24

And I replied, *Fuck you, asshole.*
And he replied, *It's in the Bible.*
And I replied, *Men wrote the damn thing.*
Did you bother to read the rest of it?

5:28 Husbands should love their wives as their own bodies ...
And he replied, *It doesn't say husbands submit.*

Still I submit to keep arguments at bay,
submit because I married the asshole who said that shit.
My mother-in-law called it compromise.
I call it my self-image's demise.

I try to end the guilty givings-in to loved ones and friends
and buck the God-ordained submission trend,
but I'll be damned if the writer's world will ever understand
how difficult it is for me to click submit .

Why not use present or enter ?

Until then, I will pretend
my poems and I are "good" wives.

THE "A" DREAM

I dreamt about him   a cute clean-shaven poet   a father   a divorcé
I thought about sex with him   in my dream   not doing-*it* thoughts

we didn't coitus   in the dream   he hired me   in my dream
to edit   to spellcheck   what the fuck do I know about commas

semicolons and colons   confusing   and   how do they make books
I can learn   it was a dream   I need another job that doesn't pay well

plus   I could use more lust in dreams or reality   earlier
not in a dream   I listened to an NPR show about Adultery in the heart

Jimmy Carter said he committed the big letter **A** in his heart
an evangelical talked about how   *it*   masturbation   not adultery

was all he was told to not think about   *it*   was wrong   poor man
said   on the radio   he spent his youth and 20s trying to train

his brain to not think about   *it*   or dream about   *it*   but   *it*
was all he obsessed about   he talked to a minister   not in the dream

at a seminary   the preacher's advice   *jerk*   *treat your member nice*
amazement and relief   *shall be thy perks*   OMG that broadcast

made me do **A**   in my brain   and   in my dreams   not in my heart
once I dreamt about a man   who had an Anaconda   for a penis

we didn't do it   in the dream   but I saw that snake
and it was big   thick   and   awesome

BREAKING RULES

There once was a lady poet
who really wasn't a lady
in the noble sense of the word
and she wasn't a grandmother
or a skillet, but she did have one
child, and she, the not-so-ladylike
poet, didn't want to cook,
but did want to write a book.

One day the wise-woman-writer
decided it was time for her poems
to be published. She revised and edited
100 pieces, printed out the entire lot,
placed them in between the bindings
of *The American Medical Association*
Encyclopedia of Medicine
and *Webster's International Dictionary*,
both interred in the inherited bookshelf
in her very cluttered yet picturesque writing space.

Now her poems are in print in books
just like books of poetry few will buy
fewer will read and to get it done
she didn't have to submit.

MY SONNET DISAPPEARED
SO HERE'S WHAT I WROTE INSTEAD

I am	so fuck-	ing mad	in-sane-	ly hot
I made	a chart	Ten syll-	a- bles	five feet.
It ran	a-way	be-fore	my eyes.	I died
in-side.	I tried	to find	by search-	ing high
and low	my doc-	u-ments,	my cloud,	my brain.
The graph	is gone.	Va-moose!	This loss,	it sucks.
I missed	my work	this day	to i-	amb write,
to learn	to be (a)	bet-ter	writ-er	of songs.
And then	I said	fuck a	foot, suck	i-ambs,
to hell	with a	pen-tam-	e-ter.	I can't,
will not	be-gin	all over	a-gain.	Will I
in-vert	or sub-	or-din-	ate? I	would rath-
er co-	or-din-	ate than	dac-tyl.	Count-er-
point and	tro-chee	might be	the best	for me.

Y OH Y?

The
yacht's
captain yaws
the yawl as
the crew yawns. We yearn
yeasty, yellow brew to share with the yeomen.
We yodel like younkers, hoot, howl and yowl as we sail to Yucatan,
eat yucca, be yuppies and dwell in yurts.

A FIBONACCI FIB

Aah
the
aardvark
exclaimed to
his partner the large
aardwolf as they neared the city
Aba that lay abaft an abandoned abattoir.
Their eyes abducted by an abnormal shimmer caused them to abort
  all abrasive
abreactions, abstaining from further absurdities that might accrue
  accusations from their companions Achates and Aeneas.

WHAT SEX ARE THEY?

I research the encyclopedia of the web
for how to sex marijuana plants.
I find pictures of minute ball sacs
and hairy white pistils the size of gnats.

Outside, with magnifying glass in hand
I stand, spread open fans and spy
with my cyclops/eagle eye
for micro-penis-like protrusions
and frog's-hair-thin threads
of trichoblasts on tits as small as tits
on a mouse on plants twice my size.

In fact, I see no sacs at all on six-foot-tall stalks
Hey plant what sex are you? I coo
as I fondle its branches. I think it's a male,
but can't tell by the feel of his skin,
yet I can't stop touching him/her/them.
Compelled to be with them
I'm in the garden more and more.

The might-be-female is beautiful.
I pinch, prune, massage stems
and lick the stick off my fingertips.
I sniff my hands and think how erotic
this obsession with sexing is, loving
two plants of unknown gender.

UDDER UPROAR

the heifer's udder sags ugly
the ultimate ultra-virus
she ululates as if her umbilicus were umbonate
unable to undulate the ungracious ungulate is untouchable
her sack unwieldy
to rise an upheaval
in an uproar
she becomes uproarious

A GAME WITH THOROUGHBREDS' NAMES

Great Minds sit on the *Glory Stone.*
Lil Allie Dancer and *King Krantz*
Catch a Glimpse of *Anna's Bandit*
hiding out in the *Majestic Harbor.*
They wait for *Sanitation* to pick up
Country Candy strewn about *Ethan's Landing.*

A *New Orleans Lady,*
dressed to *Hot Perfection,*
walks with *Cathryn Sophia.*
The strong-butted fillies swish
buxom hips to *Motown Rhythm*
when a *Mysterious Miracle* drops
White Gold from the sky, truly a *Special Treat.*

Around the far turn *Forafewdollarsmore,*
Uncle Guy buys the *Rocket Plan*
and rocket fuel for *Rocket Heat*
in hopes of finding *My Sweet Girl,*
Curalina in *Zen's Land.*

Carina Mia decides to act *Amoral*
and wanders over to *Tara's Way*
in search of country singer *Avery Glenn.*

Sheza Fine Justice for a *Paid Up Subscriber*'s
concrete company, *Zartax,* sues for a design
that stole *El Jake O's Polygram.*
Sir Genghis rescues the runaway *Home
Run Kitten* when it climbs the *Family Tree.*

But the race isn't over yet.
Conquest Stormy comes in first,
but his name is in reverse
and *Langfirst,* first, too, at the wire,
has a name so insane it must be

incorporated into a poem of nonsense
using winners' names from a May '16 Day
of racing in the US of A.

WINNERS

Each name belongs to a Thoroughbred race horse winner.

Obviously, it is a *Standard Deal*
for someone with a *Checkered Past* to get
A Wild Notion and have a glass of *Malbec*
with the *Gray Indian* while *Seeking the Light*
in the *Alabaster City*, resembling
a *Thousand Edens*, and sit by *Moonshine Bay*,
listen to a *Foxy Drummer*, watch a *Dapper Zapper*
do *Fire Tricks* with *Raging Smoke* spewing from an *Unhindered*
mouth while maintaining *Assorted Humour*. That someone
may run *Out of Patience*, plead with the *Rude Heckler*
to *Get Happy Mister* or a call might be made to the *Iron Media*
to send out a *Fashion Alert* and have the *Amazon*
escort the *Rude Heckler* to the finish line
even though they got a *Bump Start*.
The purse for first, *More Honey*.

THE WORM APOCALYPSE

Did anyone hear them squeal or were they silent in the night
as drizzle and downpours mixed with sleet rained?

Splatted on the asphalt, shoulder to shoulder, body upon body
for a half mile, not one wiggler squiggles. I know. I look. I wonder.

Did revelers in speeding cars squish them? Were they washed
out of winter's grasses? Did they crawl to the road for warmth?

I tiptoe among severed, squashed, curled, crinkled, opaque,
brownish-red and translucent pale-pink smatterings of flesh.

Were they partying when they met their demise?
What did they feel? Was this a normal occurrence?

I think of man's recent pandemic. Was this an isolated endemic?
Should I report it—*see something, say something*—and to whom?

A massacre of millions smushed into the path of my daily walk.
I search for some revelation as to why so many worms had to die?

GOOD RIDDANCE BLUES

Woke up this morning feeling lonely and blue,
wondered where your big butt had gotten off to.
Your sweet fucking ass left me no clues.

Woke up this morning couldn't get back to sleep
'cause my love for you opens wide and goes deep,
but the bed was empty of your cold, cold feet.

Woke up this morning feeling lonely and blue,
got out of bed and stepped on your shoe,
fell, hit my head and screamed like a shrew.

Woke up this morning feeling lonely and sad
cause the hole in my soul needed filling real bad.
I prayed one day I'd find me an honest lad.

Woke up this morning feeling down and dumb.
I was hung up on a good-looking bum.
I sat on the edge of the bed feeling weak and numb.

Woke up this morning feeling angry and blue.
My love wasn't enough to hold on to you,
but the itch you left pissed me off, too.

Woke up this morning, crawled out of bed,
worried how the brats and I would be fed.
You were my honey, my money, the man I wed.

This morning is past. Awake and alone
I pack your bags and cleanse this home
of all the years I worried while you roamed.

I won't wake anymore lonely, sad or blue—
instead, I'll be praising no more smell of your poo
or sounds of your blowhard cock-a-doodle-do's.

ODE TO CAT CLOUD'S MEOWS

Oh, dear cat Cloud
you are an alarm clock that will not stop.
Instead of *brrrng-brrrng* you ring
mrow, mmrrooww, mmmrrrrooowww.

Dear gray-cat Cloud,
I want others to hear what I hear,
feel what I feel; the lovely melodies
you agitate me awake with from deep sleeps.

Oh, dear noisy-gray-cat Cloud,
the long-drawn-out drawls at 3 a.m.,
your crow-like incessant meow-calls irritate
worse than the buzz of a bee flying around me.

Dear sweet-noisy-gray-cat Cloud I long to rise,
put an end to your symphonic surprises
that send me around the bend, over the edge.
I'd toss you outside if you weren't such a special friend.

Oh, dear sweet-noisy-shedding-gray-cat Cloud,
I think it shitty Mr. Kitty when you wind up the box,
sandpaper the hair off my hide with bellows
forced out from your insides. Why are you so cruel?

Oh, dear sweet-noisy-shedding-litter-missing-gray-cat Cloud,
you are so frigging loud you make it hard for me
to control me. When your voice hits the high pitches
I long to throw you in a ditch. You make me feel guilty.

Oh, dear sweet-noisy-shedding-litter-missing-dying-gray-cat Cloud,
the *mraw, mraw, mraw* someone-is-killing-me songs you sing
are the reason I keep on drinking, but I want you to know
I love you so, because you are one of God's bestest beings.

When you're gone, this poem will be the eulogy I meoww.

DOG SMELLS

The sodden massive mastiff Madeline
lumbers her ill-coordinated, fawn-colored
shedding structure through the green front door.

The stank of dank dirt, rotted compost,
waterlogged leaves, stale feces
infused with hints of ammonia
from urine drip stains under her tail
and between her hind legs, permeate
the walls and peel the flowered paper.

Lord have mercy, the big bitch smells
like a men's sweat-laden locker room,
like a feedlot for cattle being fattened
for slaughter. Rancid airs through my house.
My smeller wishes no stink slid past sensitive cilia.
The skunky sweetness offends my senses.
I abhor the not-so-subtle stenches trod
into carpets, slept in pillows,
spilled under and on seat cushions

I like less the putrid aromatics
of air fresheners so I purse my lips,
close my nostrils as much as I can
and still breathe. I shallow my intakes
and thank my senses there is only one big
smelly canine alive in this little house of mine.

THIS YARD IS MY YARD

after Woody Guthrie

This yard is my yard, this yard is my yard
from the road front to the chain-link fence line,
from concrete driveway to evergreen hedges,
this yard is made for me, not you.

When I go walking, I see large mountains
of doggy-doo from your white Samoyed.
I'm asking please keep him on your own land,
my yard is made for me, not him.

It doesn't matter that you're a neighbor
and a good one, too, I still get pissed off
when I clean poop off soles of my red boots.
This yard is made for me, not you.

I know you let that son-of-a-bitch out
to sneak on over and do his business.
Please keep his ass off my tender bluegrass,
this yard is made for me, not him.

When sun comes shining it heats his spoils.
The smell of feces makes my gut roil.
Don't let your damn dog come here anymore.
This yard is made for me, not you.

WHAT'S UP WITH UP?

The ocean is where the sky used to be.
Did they switch places while I slept?

Clouds ride the currents of wild airs beneath my feet,
curling waves ebb and flow through the sky's tides.

On wings of fins, fish fly upside down,
perch on branches of lightning, feed on stardust.

Birds swim from sea grass to ragged reefs,
undulating sogged feathers to keep from sinking,

fill bills with flying krill and plankton.
Raptors wrap talons around quail-filled clam shells.

I want to hoist my sails in the expanse above,
let the currents glide my single-masted ketch

over upside-down oceans, spread my wings—then remember
I must float up to swim, fall down to fly.

WHO'S AWAKE?

The snow falls without a sound, I am awake.
Fine as sand it rugs the ground, I am awake.

He stands at a podium, O-shaped mouth, oh gasp.
Idiocies abound. Is the world awake?

Two friends no longer speak, thanks to bigly T.
The GOP, one claims, is profound. Who's awake?

Lovers from different countries want a border wall.
They are gay, absurdities abound. Is anyone awake?

News blares in the background, Catherine stalls.
Her thoughts spin around. She wishes she wasn't awake.

WAS IT A DREAM?

I searched and walked
until my feet hurt,
in the worst shoes I owned,
the parking lot of the mega mall,
for five hours, on the hottest day
(I swear to you) of the year,
without any socks on because my feet
get so hot since I fractured my ankle
that was fixed by an ex-military doctor,
not in the parking lot or at the mega mall,
where I went because I needed new underwear,
not because I got fatter, but because clothes are so thin
and wear out or fall apart, like me, worn out
and falling apart, because I couldn't find my bamboo
pearl-colored car (what the heck is that color?),
because every handicap spot was taken
and those are the spots where I usually park
so I can find my car when I can't remember
where I parked, and then I couldn't find me,
either, on that sweltering day,
the me who can handle adversity,
not the sloppy-mess-of-sweat-and-tears me
lost in a haze in the maze of automobiles.

ACKNOWLEDGMENTS

I wish to thank the editors and publishers of the following journals, blogs and anthologies where the poems listed below appear.

"Ode to My Obesity" was posted on *booksie.com* in 2020 for a short period of time.

"The Color of Guilt," previously titled "My Feelings About Coloring or Sitting Around Wasting Time" was first posted to Lexington Poetry Month's blog in June of 2022 and was published in the 2022 LexPoMo anthology, *Locks & Bones & Bells & Stamps & Maps*, Workhorse, LLC, 2023.

"Lap Dance" was posted on Accents Publishing LexPoMo blog, 2014.

"The Joint is Jumpin'" is published in *Coming of Age, Writing and Art by Kentucky Women over 60 Volume 1*, September 2021, Red Lick Valley Press and on *Jerry Jazz Musician* online journal, Fall/Winter edition, September 2021.

"Recipe for Toe Flambé" was first published in *Circe's Lament, Anthology of Wild Women Poetry*, Accents Publishing, 2014. This is a different version of the original poem.

"Winners" was first posted on Accents Publishing LexPoMo blog website, June 2014 and in April 2023 appeared in Kentucky State Poetry Society's online edition of *Pegasus*.

"What Sex are They?" was published in Kentucky State Poetry Society's April 2023 edition of *Pegasus*.

"What's Up With Up?" was first published by Red Lick Valley Press in *Coming of Age, Writing and Art by Kentucky Women over 60, Volume 1*, September 2021.

"Was It a Dream?" was published by Paris, Kentucky's local newspaper, *The Bourbon County Citizen*, April 2019.

"Balderdash" was first published in *The Coming of Age Writing & Art by Kentucky Women Over 60, Volume 2*, Red Lick Valley Press, 2023.

"The Worm Apocalypse" was first published in *The Coming of Age Writing & Art by Kentucky Women Over 60, Volume 2*, Red Lick Valley Press, 2023

First and foremost, I want to thank Katerina Stoykova. Not only is she an excellent mentor and valuable teacher, but her belief in me and my quirky, sometimes risqué, writing enough to take a huge risk and publish this collection is proof of her kindness and courage. I embrace her with all my being.

Wayne Mackey, my husband, who has stuck with me through thick and thin, through broken bones and my lost mind, always acting like I was fine and who is still hanging in, thank you and I love you.

Olivia Perkins Mackey, thank you for choosing me to be your mother. Thank you for giving me a life beyond work, for seeing the world with me and helping me to help myself. Your strength gives me strength as I hope mine passes on to you. I will love you always.

Thank you, siblings and your partners, Michael and Judy, Toni and Stacey, and Bob and Gioia for the love, support and friendship.

Thank you, Anne Banks for encouraging me to continue my education and investing in the process. I know she won't approve of the content of this collection, but I hope she accepts her role in the journey. I will always love her and I miss our friendship more than she will ever know.

Here is an incomplete list of mentors, peers, writers and teachers who blessed me with their knowledge, guidance and support who I wish to acknowledge and thank. If I forgot you, forgive me, remember I have poor memory.

Mary Allen, Bobby Steve Baker, Sherry Chandler, Ronald Davis aka upfromsumdirt, Marta Dorton, Kathleen Gregg, Shelda Hale, Libby Falk Jones, Leatha Kendrick, George Ella Lyon, Jay McCoy, Chris McCurry, Jude McPherson, Kevin Nance, Marianne Peel Foreman, Bianca Lynne Spriggs, Eric Scott Sutherland and eight years of The Holler Poet Series and all the poets who participated in it, The Carnegie Center for Literacy and Learning, The Coming of Age group (2 seasons and about 60+ women over the age of 60), Jules Unsel, Frank X Walker, Crystal Wilkinson, Jeff Worley and Laverne Zabielski.

And to my friends, without you I would never have gotten this far in life. Thank you.

ABOUT THE AUTHOR

Catherine Perkins (she/her), poet, stand-up comedian, horse-crossing guard, zero-turn mower operator, artist, musician and semi-retired horsewoman, relocated from the east coast to Central Kentucky in 1984. Catherine and her husband, Wayne Mackey, own Perkins Mackey Stable, a Thoroughbred training and racing enterprise. Catherine has no college degrees and no awards, yet her poems appear in online journals, blogs and in numerous printed anthologies and journals.

Udder Uproar is Catherine's first published collection.

Facebook: Wackey Cathy Mackey@poetryisapassion
Instagram: Wackey Cathy Mackey (wackeycathymackey).

www.ingramcontent.com/pod-product-compliance
Lightning Source LLC
Chambersburg PA
CBHW031237120626
46545CB00003B/1168